U.S. SPECIAL FORCES

by Rachel Grack

AMICUS | AMICUS INK

Amicus High Interest is published by Amicus and Amicus Ink
P.O. Box 1329, Mankato, MN 56002
www.amicuspublishing.us

Names: Koestler-Grack, Rachel A., 1973- author.
Title: U.S. Special Forces / by Rachel Grack.
Description: Mankato, Minnesota : Amicus, [2019] | Series: Serving our
 country | Includes index. | Audience: Grades K-3.
Identifiers: LCCN 2018002411 (print) | LCCN 2018003009 (ebook) | ISBN
 9781681516035 (pdf) | ISBN 9781681515656 (library binding) | ISBN
 9781681524030 (pbk.)
Subjects: LCSH: Special forces (Military science)--United States--Juvenile
 literature.
Classification: LCC UA34.S64 (ebook) | LCC UA34.S64 K64 2019 (print) |
 DDC 356/.160973--dc23
LC record available at
 https://lccn.loc.gov/2018002411

Photo Credits: U.S. Navy Seals cover; Nikola m/Shutterstock background
pattern; Oleg Zabielin/Alamy 2; Tom Weber/Stocktrek Images/Alamy
4–5; Robert Benson/Aurora Photos/Alamy 7; US Army Photo/Alamy
8–9; Oleg Zabielin/Alamy 10–11; US Army Photo/Alamy 12–13; Chief
Photographer's Mate Andrew McKaskle/WikiCommons 14–15; US Air
Force Photo/Alamy 16; US Navy Photo/Alamy 18–19; Staff Sgt Jonathan
Snyder/age fotostock/SuperStock 20–21

Editor: Wendy Dieker
Designer: Aubrey Harper
Photo Researcher: Holly Young

Printed in China

HC 10 9 8 7 6 5 4 3 2 1
PB 10 9 8 7 6 5 4 3 2 1

TABLE OF CONTENTS

MEET THE SPECIAL FORCES

The **mission** is full of danger! It needs the strongest, smartest, and bravest. Who will go? Here come the special forces! They do what no one else dares to try.

Force Fact
Every branch of the U.S. **military** has special forces units.

TOP TRAINING

The special forces undergo hard training for their bodies and minds. They train to lug a heavy bag of gear 40 miles (64 km). Special schooling teaches them important skills. They are the best at their jobs.

ARMY RANGERS

Army Rangers are the oldest special force. They lead **raids**. They fly a helicopter deep into enemy land. Rangers drop down. It is a surprise attack! They take over the building.

GREEN BERETS

The Army Green Berets are some of the best soldiers in the world. They quietly creep close to the enemy. They strike fast with deadly aim!

Force Fact
Green Berets is a nickname. They are really called Army Special Forces.

DELTA FORCE

Delta Force is a top-secret Army unit. Not very many people know who they are. A **hostage** was freed from the enemy. Who led the way? Most likely, it was Delta Force.

NAVY SEALS

The Navy SEALs come by sea.
They sneak onto ships. They
take enemies by surprise.
Scouts swim onto shore at
night. They learn secrets about
the enemy.

Force Fact
SEAL is short for *SE*a, *A*ir, and *L*and.
SEALs are trained to work in any place.

AIR COMMANDOS

Air Force Air Commandos are on the way. They fly into danger to save troops in trouble. An American fighter jet was shot down. Air Commandos save the pilot stuck in enemy **territory.**

JOINT FORCES

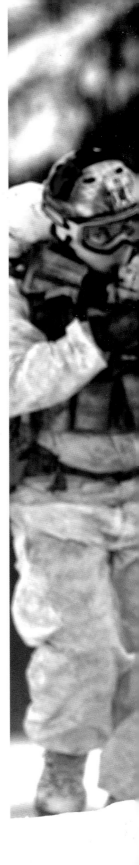

Sometimes, the top military units join forces. These are the Joint Special Operations Command. They hunt down America's scariest enemies. Their missions call for the best of the best.

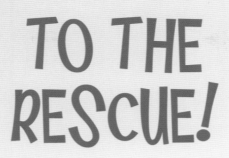

TO THE RESCUE!

The U.S. Special Forces are the nation's heroes. They face the impossible to keep America safe. No matter the danger, they are ready to come to the rescue!

U.S. SPECIAL FORCES FAST FACTS

Rangers
Military Branch: U.S. Army
Founded: modern Rangers in 1942, but Ranger units started in the Revolutionary War (1775–1783).

Green Berets
Military Branch: U.S. Army
Founded: 1952

Delta Force
Military Branch: U.S. Army
Founded: 1977

Navy SEALs
Military Branch: U.S. Navy
Founded: 1962

Air Commandos
Military Branch: U.S. Air Force
Founded: 1944

Joint Special Operations Command (JSOC)
Military Branch: Joint among all branches
Founded: 1980

WORDS TO KNOW

hostage Someone held as a prisoner as a way to get something the kidnapper wants in return for releasing the prisoner.

military The groups of armed forces that protect and defend the country.

mission A special job or task.

raid A sudden, surprise attack on a place.

scout A person who goes ahead of the group to see what's happening and bring information back to the group.

territory A wide area of land that belongs to a person or group.

LEARN MORE

Books

Bozzo, Linda. *Green Berets*. Mankato, Minn.: Amicus, 2015.

Murray, Julie. *Navy SEALs*. Minneapolis: Abdo Kids, 2015.

Slater, Lee. *Army Rangers*. Minneapolis: Abdo Publishing, 2016.

Websites

BrainPOP: Armed Forces
www.brainpop.com/socialstudies/usgovernment/armedforces/

Ducksters: United States Armed Forces
www.ducksters.com/history/us_government/united_states_armed_forces.php

INDEX

Every effort has been made to ensure that these websites are appropriate for children. However, because of the nature of the Internet, it is impossible to guarantee that these sites will remain active indefinitely or that their contents will not be altered.